THE CANADIAN LIVING
COOKING COLLECTION

VEGETABLES AND SALADS

The following Canadian companies were involved in the production
of this Collection: Colour Technologies, Fred Bird & Associates Limited,
Gordon Sibley Design Inc., On-line Graphics, Telemedia Publishing Inc. and
The Madison Book Group Inc.

We acknowledge the contribution of
Drew Warner, Joie Warner and Flavor Publications.

Produced by
The Madison Book Group Inc.
40 Madison Avenue
Toronto, Ontario
Canada
M5R 2S1

Thousand Island Dressing

This dressing is easy to prepare and makes any lettuce salad a sensation.

2 tbsp	finely chopped sweet green pepper	25 mL	
1 tbsp	finely chopped sweet red pepper	15 mL	
1 tbsp	minced fresh parsley	15 mL	
1	dill pickle, finely chopped	1	
1/2 cup	light mayonnaise	125 mL	
1/4 cup	chopped onion	50 mL	
1/4 cup	vegetable oil	50 mL	
2 tbsp	vinegar	25 mL	
2 tbsp	chili sauce	25 mL	
1 tbsp	granulated sugar	15 mL	
1 tbsp	milk	15 mL	
1	hard-cooked egg, finely chopped	1	

■ In bowl, combine green and red peppers, parsley and dill pickle. In blender, combine mayonnaise, onion, oil, vinegar, chili sauce, sugar, milk and egg; blend until smooth. Stir into vegetable mixture. Chill well. Makes about 2 cups (500 mL).

Mustard Cream Dressing

This makes a wonderful change from ordinary vinaigrette.

1/4 cup	sour cream	50 mL
1/4 cup	mayonnaise	50 mL
2 tsp	Dijon mustard	10 mL
1	clove garlic, minced	1
	Salt and pepper	

■ In small bowl, combine sour cream, mayonnaise, mustard, garlic, and salt and pepper to taste; mix well. Makes about 1/2 cup (125 mL).

Credits

Recipes in THE CANADIAN LIVING COOKING COLLECTION have been created by the *Canadian Living* Test Kitchen and by the following food writers from across Canada: **Elizabeth Baird, Karen Brown, Joanna Burkhard, James Chatto, Diane Clement, David Cohlmeyer, Pam Collacott, Bonnie Baker Cowan, Pierre Dubrulle, Eileen Dwillies, Nancy Enright, Carol Ferguson, Margaret Fraser, Susan Furlan, Anita Goldberg, Barb Holland, Patricia Jamieson, Arlene Lappin, Anne Lindsay, Lispeth Lodge, Mary McGrath, Susan Mendelson, Bernard Meyer, Beth Moffatt, Rose Murray, Iris Raven, Gerry Shikatani, Jill Snider, Kay Spicer, Linda Stephen, Bonnie Stern, Lucy Waverman, Carol White, Ted Whittaker** and **Cynny Willet.**

The full-color photographs throughout are by Canada's leading food photographers, including **Fred Bird, Doug Bradshaw, Christopher Campbell, Nino D'Angelo, Frank Grant, Michael Kohn, Suzanne McCormick, Claude Noel, John Stephens** and **Mike Visser.**

Editorial and Production Staff: Hugh Brewster, Susan Barrable, Catherine Fraccaro, Wanda Nowakowska, Sandra L. Hall, Beverley Renahan and Bernice Eisenstein.

Index

LOOK FOR THESE BESTSELLING COOKBOOKS FROM *CANADIAN LIVING*

The most trusted name in Canadian cooking

New this Fall!
CANADIAN LIVING'S COUNTRY COOKING

Rediscover the familiar tastes of country cooking at its comforting best in the pages of this beautiful full-color cookbook. Each of the more than 200 dishes featured here is brimming over with flavor and honest, great taste....*$27.00 hardcover*

THE CANADIAN LIVING COOKBOOK

Beautiful yet practical, this Canadian classic features over 525 recipes by Canada's finest food writers and a host of cooking hints, charts and ideas....*$35.00 hardcover*

THE CANADIAN LIVING LIGHT & HEALTHY COOKBOOK

Over 150 nutritious *and* delicious recipes make it easy to prepare healthy, balanced meals for the whole family. Includes handy nutrition charts for each recipe plus health and food facts....*$20.00 softcover*

THE CANADIAN LIVING MICROWAVE COOKBOOK

Over 175 delicious recipes — plus microwaving basics, charts and tips — make this an invaluable book no microwave owner should be without....*$27.00 hardcover*

THE CANADIAN LIVING RUSH-HOUR COOKBOOK

This easy-to-use cookbook features over 200 recipes and 100 menus for fast and tasty everyday meals that can be prepared in under 60 minutes. A must for today's busy cooks....*$27.00 hardcover*

THE CANADIAN LIVING BARBECUE COOKBOOK

Over 175 tested recipes for easy and delicious summer cooking plus the latest information on barbecue equipment and techniques....*$19.95 softcover*

THE CANADIAN LIVING ENTERTAINING COOKBOOK

A gorgeous gift book featuring over 350 easy-to-prepare recipes for every entertaining occasion. It includes inventive menus plus the latest ideas for setting the table — and the mood!...*$34.95 hardcover*

Also from Canadian Living
GLORIOUS CHRISTMAS CRAFTS

Over 135 imaginative ways to make Christmas extra special....*$24.95 hardcover*

All of these full-color *Canadian Living* books are available from Random House Canada in bookstores and major department stores. To order directly from *Canadian Living*, please send a cheque or money order (payable to *Canadian Living*) for the cover price (above), plus $3 shipping and handling and 7% GST on the total amount, to: *Canadian Living*, Box 220, Oakville, Ontario L6J 5A2.

VEGETABLES AND SALADS

■ *On our cover:*
Sauté of Baby
Vegetables (p. 17)

Vegetable dishes can add to the appeal of any meal. Try deliciously tender-crisp *Asparagus with Parmesan* or satisfyingly plump *Spinach-Stuffed Tomatoes* alongside your favorite main dishes. Or make a family supper with *Baked Potatoes Florentine*. Microwave directions, buying tips and serving suggestions make it extra easy to enjoy good-for-you vegetables year-round.

You'll also find your favorite salads here, like Waldorf, spinach, pasta and chicken, along with classic dressings like vinaigrette, Thousand Island and Italian. But we've also added a few twists with innovative recipes like *Warm Caesar Potato Salad*, *Zucchini Slaw*, *Salsa Salad in Lettuce Cups* and *Grilled Antipasto Salad Platter*.

Vegetables and Salads is just one of the eight full-color cookbooks that make up THE CANADIAN LIVING COOKING COLLECTION. Inside each of these colorful cookbooks are the kind of satisfying, easy-to-make dishes you'll want to cook over and over again. Each recipe in the Collection has been carefully selected and tested by *Canadian Living* to make sure it turns out wonderfully every time you make it. When you collect all eight cookbooks, you can choose from over 500 dishes — from marvelous soups to sensational desserts — all guaranteed to make any meal extra special.

Elizabeth Baird

Elizabeth Baird
Food Director, *Canadian Living* **Magazine**

Spinach-Stuffed Tomatoes

When tomatoes are at their peak, enjoy them stuffed with this mixture of spinach, mushrooms and pine nuts. Serve them with baked whole fish, roast chicken, butterflied leg of lamb, grilled pork, lamb or veal chops.

8	firm ripe tomatoes (2-1/2 lb/1 kg total)	8
	Salt	
	STUFFING	
3	pkg (each 10 oz/284 g) fresh spinach, trimmed	3
1/3 cup	butter	75 mL
2 cups	sliced mushrooms (1/2 lb/250 g)	500 mL
1/3 cup	finely chopped onion	75 mL
1 tsp	minced garlic	5 mL
1/4 lb	cream cheese, cubed	125 g
2/3 cup	pine nuts or slivered almonds	150 mL
1 tbsp	finely chopped fresh parsley	15 mL
2 tsp	chopped fresh tarragon (or 1 tsp/5 mL dried)	10 mL
2 tsp	lemon juice	10 mL
1/2 tsp	salt	2 mL
1/4 tsp	pepper	1 mL
2 tbsp	butter, melted	25 mL

■ Slice top off each tomato. Using small spoon, scoop out seeds and pulp; reserve for another use. Cut skin all around middle of each tomato to prevent splitting when baked. Sprinkle cavities lightly with salt; set upside down on rack or paper towel to drain for 30 minutes.

■ **Stuffing:** Wash spinach; shake off excess water. With just the water clinging to leaves, cook spinach, covered, in large saucepan over medium-high heat just until wilted, about 5 minutes. Drain and squeeze out as much moisture as possible; chop finely and set aside.

■ In large skillet, melt butter over medium heat; cook mushrooms, onion and garlic until softened. Increase heat to high; add spinach and cook until excess moisture evaporates. Remove from heat.

■ Mix in cream cheese, half of the pine nuts, parsley, tarragon, lemon juice, salt and pepper; taste and adjust seasoning if necessary.

■ Pat tomato cavities dry; set upright in single layer in shallow greased baking dish. Stuff each with spinach mixture and smooth surface; top with remaining pine nuts. Brush tops and sides with melted butter.

■ Cover with foil; bake in 350°F (180°C) oven for 30 minutes or until heated through but still firm. Makes 8 servings.

Lima Beans au Gratin

Try this delicious vegetable side dish and also enjoy adding varying garnishes.

2 cups	frozen lima beans	500 mL
1/4 cup	butter	50 mL
1/2 cup	chopped celery	125 mL
1/4 cup	minced onion	50 mL
1/2 cup	mayonnaise	125 mL
1/2 cup	shredded Cheddar cheese	125 mL
1 tsp	Worcestershire sauce	5 mL
1/4 cup	bread crumbs	50 mL

■ **Conventional method:** In saucepan, bring small amount of water to boil; add lima beans. Reduce heat to simmer and cook for 8 to 10 minutes or until tender; drain.

■ In saucepan, melt 2 tbsp (25 mL) of the butter over medium heat; cook celery and onion for 4 to 5 minutes or until softened. Stir in mayonnaise, 1/4 cup (50 mL) of the Cheddar and Worcestershire sauce; add lima beans.

■ **Microwave method:** In microwaveable dish, cover and microwave lima beans and 2 tbsp (25 mL) water at High for 7 minutes. Let stand for 2 minutes; drain.

■ In 4-cup (1 L) measure, microwave 2 tbsp (25 mL) of the butter at High for 1 minute. Add celery and onion; cover and microwave at High for 1 to 2 minutes or until softened. Stir in mayonnaise, 1/4 cup (50 mL) of the Cheddar and Worcestershire sauce; add lima beans.

■ **Both methods:** Transfer to 6-cup (1.5 L) baking dish. Combine remaining butter, Cheddar and bread crumbs; sprinkle over lima beans. Broil for 2 to 3 minutes or until cheese has melted and topping is golden. Makes 4 servings.

Brighten up cooked lima beans with simple additions such as chopped fresh parsley, diced onion, finely chopped tomatoes, mustard or paprika.

Stir-Fry of Bok Choy, Carrots, Cauliflower and Broccoli

Sometimes called Chinese cabbage, mild-flavored bok choy is a pleasing addition to a stir-fry, soup or salad. Add any seasonal vegetables to this stir-fry.

1 tbsp	vegetable oil	15 mL
2 cups	cauliflower florets	500 mL
2 cups	broccoli florets	500 mL
1-1/2 cups	sliced carrots	375 mL
1/2 cup	chicken stock	125 mL
1/4 lb	snow peas, trimmed	125 g
1/2 lb	bok choy, cut in 1-1/2-inch (4 cm) pieces	250 g
1 tbsp	minced gingerroot	15 mL
1 tsp	minced garlic	5 mL
1 tbsp	soy sauce	15 mL
	Salt and pepper	

■ In wok or large nonstick skillet, heat oil over medium heat; stir-fry cauliflower, broccoli and carrots for 3 minutes. Add stock; cover and steam for 2 minutes.

■ Add snow peas; stir-fry for 1 minute. Add bok choy, gingerroot and garlic; stir-fry for 1 to 2 minutes or until vegetables are tender-crisp. Stir in soy sauce. Season with salt and pepper to taste. Makes 4 to 6 servings.

Ginger Orange Squash

Zesty and satisfying, this flavored squash is perfect with roast beef or chicken on a cold wintery day.

3 cups	frozen cubed squash	750 mL
2 tbsp	butter	25 mL
2 tbsp	orange juice	25 mL
1 tsp	grated orange rind	5 mL
1/4 tsp	each salt and ginger	1 mL
Pinch	each nutmeg and pepper	Pinch

■ **Conventional method:** In saucepan, bring small amount of water to boil; add squash. Reduce heat to simmer and cook for 6 minutes or until tender; drain.

■ **Microwave method:** In microwaveable dish, cover and microwave squash and 2 tbsp (25 mL) water at High for 6 minutes. Let stand for 2 minutes; drain.

■ **Both methods:** Mash squash; beat in butter, orange juice and rind, salt, ginger, nutmeg and pepper. Makes 4 servings.

Maple Butter Carrots

Carrots with a delectable twist, this dish will go around the table for second helpings.

3 cups	frozen sliced carrots	750 mL
2 tbsp	butter	25 mL
1/4 cup	maple syrup	50 mL
1 tsp	lemon juice	5 mL
1/2 tsp	salt	2 mL

■ **Conventional method:** In saucepan, bring small amount of water to boil; add carrots. Reduce heat to simmer and cook for 8 minutes or until tender; drain.

■ In saucepan, melt butter over medium heat. Stir in maple syrup, lemon juice and salt; bring to boil. Pour over carrots.

■ **Microwave method:** In microwaveable dish, cover and microwave carrots and 2 tbsp (25 mL) water at High for 9 minutes. Let stand for 2 minutes; drain.

■ In 2-cup (500 mL) measure, microwave butter at High for 1 minute. Stir in maple syrup, lemon juice and salt; microwave until boiling. Pour over carrots.

■ Makes 4 servings.

VEGETABLE DRESS-UPS

The addition of a little lemon juice and brown sugar zips up the flavor of cooked squash. Or add a touch of maple syrup for a great flavor combination.

• Dress up cooked carrots with a sprinkling of chopped fresh parsley, rosemary or dill. Chopped walnuts or pecans can add flavorful crunch.

Asparagus with Parmesan

When you buy asparagus, look for stalks of equal thickness so they cook in the same length of time.

2 lb	asparagus	1 kg
1 tsp	salt	5 mL
1/4 tsp	pepper	1 mL
3/4 cup	freshly grated Parmesan cheese	175 mL
1/4 cup	cold butter, cut in pieces	50 mL

■ Trim 1 inch (2.5 cm) from asparagus stalk; peel 2 inches (5 cm) of stalk if tough.

■ In large skillet of boiling water, cook asparagus until barely tender, 3 to 6 minutes.

■ In greased 13- × 9-inch (3.5 L) shallow casserole, arrange asparagus in single layer. Season with salt and pepper. Sprinkle with cheese; dot with butter. *(Recipe can be prepared to this point, covered and kept at room temperature for up to 3 hours.)*

■ Bake in 350°F (180°C) oven for 20 minutes or until asparagus is heated through and cheese is melted. Makes 6 to 8 servings.

ASPARAGUS — A SURE SIGN OF SPRING!

Tall and proud in the produce section, Canadian asparagus is a great sign of spring.

• Select firm, straight, rich green spears that are uniform in size and have closed tips. Stalks should be well rounded: ridges are a sign of age. The thicker the spear, the tastier and more tender it is.

• Refrigerate for up to three days by wrapping the base of the stalks in damp paper towels and placing them in a plastic bag.

Or, stand them in 1 inch (2.5 cm) of water and cover with a plastic bag.

• Brush gently under cold running water to remove sand. Hold spear with both hands and snap off end; the stalk will break at the point where toughness stops.

• Cook asparagus by laying spears in wide saucepan of boiling salted water and cooking for 3 to 6 minutes or until tender-crisp. Or, cook in steamer basket over boiling water for the same time.

Microwave Spiced Red Cabbage

This sweet-and-sour side dish goes well with any kind of meat — especially pork chops, sausages or roasted meats.

Half	head red cabbage	Half
1/3 cup	white vinegar	75 mL
1 tbsp	granulated sugar	15 mL
4	whole cloves	4
4	peppercorns	4
1	bay leaf	1
2 tsp	coriander seeds	10 mL
1 tbsp	butter	15 mL
1	onion, finely chopped	1
1	large tart apple, peeled and sliced	1
	Salt and pepper	

■ Finely slice cabbage; place in large bowl. Mix together vinegar and sugar; stir into cabbage. In double thickness square of cheesecloth, tie together cloves, peppercorns, bay leaf and coriander seeds; add to cabbage mixture. Let stand for at least 15 minutes or up to 1 hour to blend flavors.

■ In 12-cup (3 L) microwaveable dish, microwave butter at High for 10 to 30 seconds or until melted. Stir in onion; microwave at High for 1 minute.

■ Stir in cabbage mixture along with apple; cover and microwave at High for 20 minutes or until cabbage is tender, stirring every 5 minutes. Remove cheesecloth bag. Season with salt and pepper to taste. Makes 4 to 6 servings.

THE CABBAGE PATCH

When buying cabbage (green, red, savoy and bok choy), look for firm heads, heavy for their size; leaves should have bright color and be free of blemishes, signs of worms and wilting.

• To cook: Trim outer leaves and discard core. Cut into wedges or shred. Boil, steam, stir-fry or braise green or Savoy cabbage or bok choy until tender-crisp. Red cabbage requires longer cooking and the addition of a little lemon juice or vinegar to keep its bright color. Good raw.

Stir-Fried Broccoli and Red Peppers

This colorful stir-fry goes well with broiled chicken or fish.

1 tbsp	sesame seeds	15 mL
2 tbsp	vegetable oil	25 mL
1 tsp	sesame oil	5 mL
2 tsp	minced garlic	10 mL
1 tsp	finely chopped gingerroot	5 mL
1	large onion, sliced	1
1	bunch broccoli, cut in bite-size pieces	1
1	large sweet red pepper, sliced	1
1/2 lb	small mushrooms	250 g
1/3 cup	chicken stock	75 mL
2 tsp	cornstarch	10 mL
2 tsp	soy sauce	10 mL

■ Add onion and broccoli; stir-fry for 1 minute. Add red pepper and mushrooms; stir-fry for 2 minutes. Add half of the stock; cover and steam for 1 to 2 minutes or until broccoli is tender-crisp.

■ Stir together remaining stock, cornstarch and soy sauce; pour over vegetables, tossing for about 30 seconds to gloss. Sprinkle with toasted sesame seeds. Makes 6 servings.

■ In skillet over medium heat, toast sesame seeds, stirring frequently, for 8 to 10 minutes or until brown; set aside.

■ In wok or large skillet, heat vegetable oil and sesame oil over high heat; stir-fry garlic and ginger-root for 30 seconds. Remove with slotted spoon and discard.

Beans with Fresh Tomato and Fennel Sauce

This savory side dish makes a good accompaniment to grilled fish.

2 tbsp	olive oil	25 mL
1/2 cup	finely chopped onion	125 mL
1	large clove garlic, minced	1
1-1/2 cups	diced seeded peeled tomatoes	375 mL
1/2 tsp	fennel seeds	2 mL
1/4 tsp	salt	1 mL
Pinch	each pepper and granulated sugar	Pinch
1 lb	green beans	500 g
1/4 cup	finely chopped fresh parsley	50 mL

■ In large saucepan, heat oil over medium heat; cook onion and garlic until softened, about 2 minutes.

■ Stir in tomatoes, fennel seeds, salt, pepper and sugar; cook, uncovered and stirring often, until thickened and juices have evaporated, about 10 minutes. Taste and adjust seasoning if necessary.

■ Meanwhile, trim beans. In large saucepan of boiling salted water, cook beans until tender-crisp, 5 to 8 minutes. Drain; toss with sauce and parsley. Makes about 4 servings.

BEAN BASICS

Top, tail and rinse 1 lb (500 g) green beans, enough for 4 servings.

• *Bring large saucepan of salted water to full rolling boil. Add beans, bring back to boil and boil hard for 5 to 8 minutes or until beans are tender-crisp. Drain and season with salt, a pat of butter and a squirt of lemon juice, or use one of the Simple Flourishes.*

• *To microwave, combine beans with 1/2 cup (125 mL) water or chicken stock in microwaveable dish. Microwave, covered, at High for 10 to 14 minutes. Let stand for 1 to 2 minutes or until beans are tender-crisp before seasoning as desired.*

SIMPLE FLOURISHES

Toss 1 lb (500 g) cooked green beans with any of these flavorful finales.

• *Sauté 1/4 cup (50 mL) chopped pecans in 2 tbsp (25 mL) butter. Add 3 tbsp (50 mL) orange juice, pinch of mace, and salt and pepper to taste. Boil for 30 seconds.*

• *Combine 2 tbsp (25 mL) melted butter, 2 tbsp (25 mL) chopped chives, 2 tsp (10 mL) chopped fresh mint or sage, and salt and pepper to taste.*

• *Fry 1 tbsp (15 mL) slivered almonds in 2 tbsp (25 mL) vegetable oil until golden. Add 1/2 tsp (2 mL) minced gingerroot, 1 minced clove garlic, 1-1/2 tsp (7 mL) light soy sauce and 1/4 tsp (1 mL) sesame oil.*

• *Fry 1 large minced clove garlic in 2 tbsp (25 mL) olive oil briefly. Add 1 tsp (5 mL) lemon juice, 1/2 tsp (2 mL) chopped fresh savory, and salt and pepper to taste.*

• *Combine 1 tbsp (15 mL) melted butter, 1/4 cup (50 mL) freshly grated Parmesan cheese, and salt and pepper to taste.*

Cauliflower with Fresh Dill

*Fresh dill is particularly good with cauliflower. However, you can use 2 tbsp
(25 mL) chopped fresh thyme, marjoram, savory, oregano or basil or 1 tsp (5 mL)
dried thyme or basil instead. A chopped tomato can be added for color. Any
leftovers are delicious served cold.*

1	head cauliflower, cut in florets	1
2 tbsp	lemon juice	25 mL
2 tbsp	vegetable oil	25 mL
	Salt and pepper	
1/4 cup	chopped fresh dill	50 mL
2 tbsp	chopped fresh parsley	25 mL
1 tbsp	minced chives or green onions	15 mL

■ In large pot of boiling water, cover and cook cauliflower until tender-crisp, 10 to 15 minutes. Drain and place in warmed serving dish.

■ Mix lemon juice with oil; pour over cauliflower and toss gently. Season with salt and pepper to taste. Sprinkle with dill, parsley and chives. Makes 4 to 6 servings.

BUYING AND COOKING CAULIFLOWER
Look for compact, firm, white to creamy-white florets; avoid any that are trimmed or brownish. Base should look freshly cut. Leaves should be firm and green.
• To cook: Remove leaves and stem. Use whole or cut into florets. Add 1 tbsp (15 mL) lemon juice or vinegar to boiling water to preserve white color; or steam, stir-fry or microwave. Good raw.

Sauté of Baby Vegetables

This mixture of vegetables looks spectacular and tastes wonderful. You can blanch the vegetables ahead of time.

1 lb	baby carrots, peeled	500 g
1/2 lb	pearl onions (about 2 cups/500 mL)	250 g
1/4 cup	unsalted butter	50 mL
2	cloves garlic, minced	2
1 tsp	finely chopped gingerroot	5 mL
2 cups	cherry tomatoes	500 mL
1 tsp	salt	5 mL
1/4 tsp	pepper	1 mL
	Chopped fresh chives	

■ Add onions to pot; cook for 2 minutes or until tender-crisp and transfer to ice water. Drain onions and carrots; peel onions.

■ In large skillet, melt butter over medium-low heat; cook garlic and gingerroot, stirring, for 3 minutes or until fragrant but not browned. Increase heat to medium-high.

■ Add carrots, onions and tomatoes, stirring to coat; cook for about 3 minutes or until heated through. Sprinkle with salt and pepper; garnish with chives. Makes 4 to 6 servings.

■ In pot of boiling water, cook carrots for about 5 minutes or until tender-crisp. With slotted spoon, transfer to ice water to stop cooking.

Mexican Corn

This colorful dish of green, red and yellow is as tasty as it looks.

2 cups	frozen corn	500 mL
2 tbsp	butter	25 mL
1/4 cup	diced onion	50 mL
1/4 cup	diced sweet green pepper	50 mL
2 tbsp	chopped pimiento	25 mL
1/2 tsp	salt	2 mL
1/4 tsp	pepper	1 mL

■ **Conventional method:** In saucepan, bring small amount of water to boil; add corn. Reduce heat to simmer and cook for 5 to 7 minutes or until tender; drain.

■ Meanwhile, in saucepan, melt butter over medium heat; cook onion and green pepper for 2 to 3 minutes or until softened. Stir in pimiento, salt, pepper and corn.

■ **Microwave method:** In microwaveable dish, cover and microwave corn and 2 tbsp (25 mL) water at High for 5 minutes. Let stand for 2 minutes; drain.

■ In microwaveable bowl, microwave butter at High for 1 minute. Add onion and green pepper; cover and microwave at High for 1 to 2 minutes or until softened. Stir in pimiento, salt, pepper and corn.

■ Makes 4 servings.

Peas in Creamy Mushroom Sauce

For a vegetarian meal, try serving this savory sauce with your favorite noodles.

2 cups	frozen peas	500 mL
2 tbsp	butter	25 mL
1 cup	sliced mushrooms	250 mL
1 tbsp	all-purpose flour	15 mL
1 cup	milk or light cream	250 mL
1/4 tsp	each salt and pepper	1 mL
Pinch	nutmeg	Pinch

■ **Conventional method:** In saucepan, bring small amount of water to boil; add peas. Reduce heat to simmer and cook for 4 to 5 minutes or until tender; drain.

■ Meanwhile, in saucepan, melt butter over medium heat; cook mushrooms for 2 minutes.

Sprinkle with flour; cook for 1 minute, stirring constantly. Whisk in milk, salt, pepper and nutmeg; cook for about 4 minutes or until smooth and thickened. Stir in peas.

■ **Microwave method:** In microwaveable dish, cover and microwave peas and 2 tbsp (25 mL) water at High for 5 minutes. Let stand for 2 minutes; drain.

■ In 4-cup (1 L) microwaveable measure, microwave butter at High for 1 minute. Add mushrooms; cover and cook for about 2 minutes or until tender, stirring once. Stir in flour; whisk in milk until smooth. Microwave at High for 2 to 3 minutes or until smooth and thickened, stirring once. Add salt, pepper and nutmeg; stir in peas.

■ Makes 4 servings.

SIMPLE SEASONINGS
As a quick seasoning for cooked peas, add some chopped fresh parsley, dill or mint. Or combine the peas with sautéed sliced green onions, celery or mushrooms.
• Add color and flavor to simply cooked corn by tossing it with cooked bacon bits or chopped sweet red and green peppers.

Corn on the Cob with Flavored Butters

For full appreciation of its wonderful flavor, corn should be served as a separate course. Enhance it with flavored butters, and serve it with thick slices of beefsteak tomatoes and fresh Italian bread.

12	cobs corn, husked	12
	Flavored Butters (recipes follow)	

■ In large pot of boiling water, cook corn for at least 3 minutes or up to 10 minutes, depending on size and tenderness, or until tender. Drain and serve with choice of Flavored Butters. Makes 6 servings.

FLAVORED BUTTERS

Chili Butter: Combine 1/2 cup (125 mL) softened butter, 1 tsp (5 mL) chili powder, 1 tsp (5 mL) salt and 1/4 tsp (1 mL) pepper.

Onion Butter: Combine 1/2 cup (125 mL) softened butter, 2 finely chopped green onions, 1 tsp (5 mL) salt and 1/4 tsp (1 mL) pepper.

Parsley Butter: Combine 1/2 cup (125 mL) softened butter, 2 tbsp (25 mL) chopped fresh parsley, 1 tsp (5 mL) salt and 1/4 tsp (1 mL) pepper.

Dill Butter: Combine 1/2 cup (125 mL) softened butter, 2 tsp (10 mL) chopped fresh dill or 3/4 tsp (4 mL) dried dillweed, 1 tsp (5 mL) salt and 1/4 tsp (1 mL) pepper.

BARBECUED CORN ON THE COB
This is an easy method for cooking corn on the barbecue. Kernels stay moist and firm and have a dewy, fresh-picked taste.
• Peel back husks, leaving them attached at the base; remove all silk. Rewrap corn in husks and secure with string. Soak cobs in cold water for 15 minutes or remove husks and silk and just wrap cobs in foil.
• Grill cobs 4 inches (10 cm) from hot coals or on high setting, turning occasionally, for 25 minutes or until tender when pierced with fork.

Purée of Leeks

This beautiful green purée is a sensation, both to the eye and the taste buds. It's the perfect companion for grilled chicken, fish or liver.

8	leeks	8
1/4 cup	butter	50 mL
1/3 cup	whipping cream	75 mL
1/4 tsp	each salt and pepper	1 mL
1/4 tsp	mace	1 mL

■ Trim leeks and slit lengthwise; spread leaves and rinse thoroughly under cold water to flush out grit. Chop leeks finely.

■ In heavy saucepan, melt butter over medium-low heat; cook leeks, covered and stirring occasionally, until wilted and tender, about 20 minutes. Increase heat to medium-high; cook, uncovered and stirring frequently, for 10 minutes to evaporate some of the liquid.

■ In food processor or blender, purée leeks until fairly smooth; return to clean saucepan. Stir in cream, salt, pepper and mace; heat through for 3 or 4 minutes. Taste and adjust seasoning. Makes 6 servings.

Leeks are often used in soups or in combination with other vegetables. Onions can be used as a substitute when leeks are not available or you don't have any on hand. We've given them centre stage in our recipe for Purée of Leeks.

Honey-Glazed Rutabaga or Turnip

The next time you roast a turkey or capon, serve it with this easy-to-make side dish, which has the pleasant sweetness of honey.

2 lb	rutabaga or turnips, peeled	1 kg
2 tbsp	butter	25 mL
1/4 cup	liquid honey	50 mL
1/4 tsp	ginger	1 mL
	Salt and pepper	

■ Cut rutabaga into 1/2-inch (1 cm) thick slices. Halve or quarter slices if large. In saucepan of boiling salted water, cook rutabaga for 15 minutes (turnips for 8 minutes) or just until tender. Drain.

■ Immediately stir in butter; cook over high heat, shaking pan often, for 1 minute or until slices are coated. Stir in honey and ginger; cook, stirring often, for 1 minute or until glazed. Season with salt and pepper to taste. Makes 4 servings.

Rutabaga and Pear Purée

This creamy vegetable purée, delightfully sweetened with pear, can be made ahead and gently reheated before serving. Add the sour cream or yogurt when reheating.

1	**small rutabaga or yellow turnip (1-1/4 lb/625 g), peeled and cubed**	1
1	**ripe pear, peeled, cored and cut in chunks**	1
1/4 cup	**sour cream or plain yogurt**	50 mL
1 tbsp	**butter**	15 mL
Pinch	**nutmeg**	Pinch
	Salt and pepper	

■ In steamer over boiling water, steam rutabaga for 15 minutes or until nearly tender. Add pear; cook for 5 to 10 minutes or until rutabaga is tender. Drain well.

■ In food processor or blender, purée rutabaga mixture until smooth. (Alternatively, mash or push through food mill.) Add sour cream, butter, nutmeg, and salt and pepper to taste; process just until combined. Reheat in saucepan over medium-low heat or in microwave until heated through. Makes about 4 servings.

Zucchini Basil Toss

Don't overcook the zucchini — it should be a crisp contrast to any main course.

4	**small zucchini (about 1-1/4 lb/625 g total)**	4
1/4 cup	**pine nuts or slivered almonds**	50 mL
4 tsp	**olive oil**	20 mL
2	**cloves garlic, minced**	2
2 tbsp	**chopped fresh basil (or 2 tsp/10 mL dried)**	25 mL
	Salt and pepper	
1/4 cup	**freshly grated Parmesan cheese**	50 mL

■ Cut zucchini into matchstick-size pieces; set aside. In skillet, toast pine nuts over medium heat, stirring constantly, for about 3 minutes or until golden. Remove and set aside.

■ Add oil to skillet and heat; cook zucchini, garlic and basil, stirring often, for 2 to 4 minutes or until tender-crisp. Season with salt and pepper to taste. Transfer to warmed bowl; sprinkle with cheese and nuts. Makes 4 servings.

Potato and Mushroom Gratin Savoyard

A gratin savoyard is a classy cheesy version of scalloped potatoes made with chicken stock instead of milk and with mushrooms added.

1/4 cup	butter, softened	50 mL
2 cups	sliced mushrooms (about 6 oz/175 g)	500 mL
1 tbsp	finely chopped onion	15 mL
1	clove garlic, halved	1
2	eggs	2
2 cups	chicken stock	500 mL
2 tbsp	all-purpose flour	25 mL
1/2 tsp	salt	2 mL
1/4 tsp	each nutmeg and pepper	1 mL
6 cups	thinly sliced peeled potatoes (2 lb/1 kg)	1.5 L
1 cup	shredded Gruyère cheese	250 mL
	TOPPING	
1 cup	shredded Gruyère cheese	250 mL
1/4 cup	coarse dry bread crumbs	50 mL

■ In large skillet, melt 2 tbsp (25 mL) of the butter over medium heat; cook mushrooms and onion until tender and moisture has evaporated, 5 to 8 minutes. Set aside.

■ Rub inside of 11- × 7-inch (2 L) baking dish firmly with cut sides of garlic; discard garlic. Spread remaining butter over inside of dish.

■ Whisk together eggs, stock, flour, salt, nutmeg and pepper; set aside. Combine potatoes and cheese; spread half in prepared dish. Spread mushroom mixture over top. Arrange remaining potato mixture in layers of overlapping slices on top. Pour egg mixture over, lifting slices to allow even distribution.

■ **Topping:** Combine cheese and crumbs; sprinkle over potatoes. Bake in 300°F (150°C) oven for 2 hours or until potatoes are tender and egg mixture is set. Serve immediately. Makes 6 to 8 servings.

> *NEW POTATOES*
>
> *There's nothing better than the small, moist new potatoes of summer. These red or tan-skinned potatoes are best simply boiled or steamed with their skins on and served with a dusting of salt and a sprinkle of chopped fresh dill and parsley. Because new potatoes are dug while immature, they retain a lot of moisture; this waxy texture makes them ideal for potato salads and pan-frying.*

Greek New Potato Skewers

If you know you'll be really short for time, plan ahead by cooking extra potatoes with supper the night before. If you can't find tiny new potatoes, quarter four larger ones. If using wooden skewers, soak them for 30 minutes first.

16	tiny new potatoes (about 1 lb/500 g)	16
2 tbsp	olive oil	25 mL
1 tbsp	chopped fresh oregano (or 1 tsp/5 mL dried)	15 mL
1	clove garlic, minced	1
1/2 tsp	salt	2 mL
Pinch	pepper	Pinch
Pinch	hot pepper flakes	Pinch
2	plum tomatoes, quartered	2
1	sweet green pepper, cut in 16 chunks	1

■ In large pot of boiling water, cook potatoes until tender, about 10 minutes; drain.

■ In bowl, stir together oil, oregano, garlic, salt, pepper and hot pepper flakes; add potatoes, tomatoes and green pepper, stirring to coat evenly.

■ Alternating vegetables, thread each of 4 skewers with 4 potatoes, 2 tomato wedges and 4 green pepper chunks. Cook on greased grill for 4 to 6 minutes or until potato skins are crisp, turning often and brushing with any remaining oil mixture. Makes 4 servings.

No-Fry French Fries

Choose mature potatoes suitable for baking when making these oven French fries.

4	**potatoes** **(1-1/2 lb/750 g total)**	4
2 tbsp	**vegetable oil**	25 mL
	Salt	

■ Peel potatoes; cut lengthwise into sticks about 1/2 inch (1 cm) thick. Soak in bowl of ice water for 15 minutes. Drain thoroughly and pat dry.

■ On large baking sheet, arrange potatoes in single layer; drizzle with oil. Turn potatoes to coat all sides.

■ Bake, turning occasionally, in 450°F (230°C) oven for 30 to 35 minutes or until golden brown and crisp. Sprinkle with salt. Makes 4 servings.

(clockwise from top left) Baked Potatoes Florentine (p. 27); Potato and Mushroom Gratin Savoyard (p. 24); No-Fry French Fries ▲

Baked Potatoes Florentine

Potatoes stuffed with this spinach and mushroom mixture are fancy enough for a dinner party, yet satisfying enough for family suppers or weekend lunches.

6	baking potatoes	6
1	pkg (10 oz/284 g) fresh spinach, trimmed	1
1/4 cup	butter	50 mL
1/3 cup	finely chopped onion	75 mL
1/2 cup	finely chopped mushrooms	125 mL
1 tsp	salt	5 mL
1/2 tsp	chopped fresh rosemary (or 1/4 tsp/1 mL dried)	2 mL
1/4 tsp	pepper	1 mL
1/2 cup	plain yogurt	125 mL
1/2 cup	mayonnaise	125 mL
	TOPPING	
2 tbsp	butter	25 mL
1/2 cup	bread crumbs from day-old homemade-style bread	125 mL
1/4 cup	slivered or sliced almonds	50 mL

■ Scrub potatoes. Prick with fork and bake in 400°F (200°C) oven until potatoes yield when gently squeezed, 45 to 55 minutes.

■ Meanwhile, rinse spinach; shake off excess water. With just the water clinging to leaves, cover and cook spinach just until wilted, 3 to 4 minutes. Drain and squeeze out as much moisture as possible; chop finely and set aside.

■ In large skillet, melt butter over medium heat; cook onion for 2 minutes. Stir in mushrooms, salt, rosemary and pepper; cook gently for 3 to 4 minutes or until vegetables are tender. Mix in spinach; set aside.

■ Cut slice from top of each potato. Scoop out pulp to bowl, leaving 1/4-inch (5 mm) thick shell. Mash pulp; stir in spinach mixture, yogurt and mayonnaise. Taste and adjust seasoning if necessary. Spoon mixture into potato shells and smooth tops. Place on oven-proof platter.

■ **Topping:** In skillet, melt butter; sauté bread crumbs and almonds for a few minutes or just until crisp and golden. Sprinkle evenly over potatoes. Bake in 400°F (200°C) oven until potatoes are heated through and topping is crisp, 15 to 20 minutes. Makes 6 servings.

Microwave Scalloped Potatoes

These potatoes are fast and by pairing the microwave with your broiler, you get a wonderful golden topping.

3 tbsp	butter	50 mL
3 tbsp	all-purpose flour	50 mL
1-1/2 cups	milk	375 mL
3/4 tsp	salt	4 mL
1/2 tsp	dry mustard	2 mL
1/4 tsp	pepper	1 mL
1/4 cup	freshly grated Parmesan cheese	50 mL
4	potatoes, peeled and sliced	4
3	green onions, sliced	3
3/4 cup	shredded Swiss cheese	175 mL

■ In 8-cup (2 L) microwaveable measure, microwave butter at High for 30 to 40 seconds or until melted; whisk in flour.

■ Stir in milk, salt, mustard and pepper; microwave, uncovered, at High for 3 to 5 minutes or until boiling and thickened, stirring twice. Stir in Parmesan.

■ In 8-cup (2 L) shallow microwaveable oven-proof casserole, spread half of the potatoes; stir in sauce to coat. Add onions and remaining potatoes; mix well, building up sides higher than centre for more even cooking.

■ Cover and microwave at High for 18 to 22 minutes or until potatoes are tender, rotating dish twice. Sprinkle with Swiss cheese. Broil for 3 to 5 minutes or until cheese is melted and golden. Let stand for 5 minutes. Makes 4 servings.

Tuscan Potatoes with Peppers

Italian cooks combine potatoes and peppers in a variety of ways. Some people add zucchini and others, as in the recipe below, add tomatoes for a harvest vegetable ragout. Serve with roast lamb, baked chicken, Italian sausages, fish or liver.

2 tbsp	olive oil	25 mL
1 cup	chopped onions	250 mL
1	large clove garlic, minced	1
1	large sweet pepper, cut in 1-inch (2.5 cm) chunks	1
3	large potatoes, cut in 1-inch (2.5 cm) cubes (about 1 lb/500 g)	3
1-1/2 cups	chopped seeded peeled tomatoes	375 mL
1/2 tsp	chopped fresh rosemary or oregano (or 1/4 tsp/1 mL dried)	2 mL
	Salt and pepper	
1/4 cup	chicken stock or water (optional)	50 mL

■ In heavy saucepan or deep skillet, heat oil over medium heat; cook onions and garlic for 3 minutes without browning.

■ Add sweet pepper and potatoes, stirring to coat evenly. Cover and cook over low heat for 10 minutes.

■ Stir in tomatoes, rosemary, and salt and pepper to taste. (If mixture appears dry, add stock.) Cover and cook, stirring periodically, for about 15 minutes or until vegetables are tender. Makes 4 servings.

ONE POTATO, TWO POTATO...
Store potatoes in a cool (45 to 50°F/7 to 10°C), dark, well-ventilated place. Potatoes kept in a warmer place, such as under your kitchen sink, may sprout and shrivel. If you don't have an ideal place to store potatoes, buy only what you can consume within a few days.

• If potatoes have been stored in a place that's colder than 40°F (5°C), the starch changes to sugar and the potatoes may taste slightly sweet. If you know the potatoes have been in a storage area this cold, let them stand for a few days at room temperature to allow the sugar to change back into starch.

Make-Ahead Broccoli

When you're entertaining guests, the last-minute cooking of green vegetables can be a problem. One way to master the split-second timing required for perfect bright green broccoli is to partially cook it in advance, then blanch it briefly just before serving.

1	bunch broccoli	1
2 tbsp	vegetable oil or butter, melted	25 mL
2	cloves garlic, minced (optional)	2
3 tbsp	lemon juice	50 mL
1/4 tsp	salt	1 mL
Pinch	pepper	Pinch
	Sliced pitted black olives (optional)	

■ Trim and peel broccoli stalks; cut into 1/2-inch (1 cm) thick pieces. Separate top into florets.

■ In large pot of boiling water, cook broccoli for 3 to 5 minutes or just until tender-crisp. Immediately drain and plunge into large bowl of ice water. Drain and wrap in paper towels; refrigerate for up to 1 day.

■ In small skillet, heat oil over medium-low heat; cook garlic (if using) for 1 minute. Add lemon juice, salt and pepper.

■ Meanwhile, blanch broccoli in boiling water for 1 minute; drain throughly and toss with lemon juice mixture. Transfer to warm serving dish; sprinkle with olives (if using). Makes about 6 servings.

BUYING AND COOKING BROCCOLI
Look for firm compact clusters of small flower buds and thin stalks; they should be dark blue-green. Avoid yellow or limp heads and split bottom stalks.
• To cook: Trim stalks and remove leaves. Peel stalks if desired. Cut into smaller pieces and florets or leave large. Eat raw in salads or with dips, or boil, steam, stir-fry or microwave until tender-crisp.

Brussels Sprouts with Red Pepper and Potatoes

Potatoes — new or old, red or white, sliced, quartered or cubed — and colorful sweet red pepper are a winning combination when teamed with brussels sprouts.

2 tbsp	butter	25 mL
1	onion, chopped	1
1	large potato, peeled and cubed	1
1	bay leaf	1
1 lb	brussels sprouts (halved if large)	500 g
1	sweet red pepper, cut in 1/2-inch (1 cm) pieces	1
1/4 cup	chicken or vegetable stock	50 mL
	Salt and pepper	
2 tbsp	chopped fresh parsley or green onions	25 mL

■ In large nonstick skillet, melt butter over medium heat; cook onion, potato and bay leaf, stirring often, until onion is tender, 2 to 3 minutes.

■ Add brussels sprouts, red pepper and stock; cover and cook for about 10 minutes or until brussels sprouts and potatoes are tender. Remove bay leaf. Season with salt and pepper to taste. Sprinkle with parsley. Makes 6 servings.

Mashed Potatoes

Mash potatoes with a variety of fall vegetables to make hearty family dishes.

6	**potatoes, peeled (1-3/4 lb/875 g total)**	6
	Vegetable Twists (recipes follow)	
3/4 cup	**hot milk**	175 mL
1/4 cup	**finely chopped fresh parsley**	50 mL
1/4 cup	**butter**	50 mL
	Salt and pepper	

■ In saucepan of lightly salted boiling water, cook potatoes until tender. Drain and return pan to heat, shaking for a few seconds to dry potatoes. Mash smoothly or put through ricer.

Mix in one of the Vegetable Twists; blend in milk, parsley, butter, and salt and pepper to taste. Makes 6 to 8 servings.

VEGETABLE TWISTS

Carrot-Onion: Peel and chop 6 carrots and 2 onions. Cook in saucepan of boiling salted water until tender; drain and purée.

Rutabaga: Peel and chop one 1-1/2-lb (750 g) rutabaga. Cook in saucepan of boiling salted water until tender; drain and purée.

Parsnip: Peel and chop 9 small parsnips (1-1/4 lb/655 g total). Cook in saucepan of boiling salted water until tender; drain and purée.

Cabbage-Bacon: Combine 8 cups (2 L) cooked finely chopped cabbage with 4 strips cooked and crumbled bacon.

Lots of Onions

This is marvellous with roast beef, pork and barbecued meats. The long oven-braising brings out the sweetness and intensity of the onion flavor.

2 lb	**onions, thickly sliced (about 12)**	1 kg
2 tbsp	**ketchup**	25 mL
2 tbsp	**water**	25 mL
1 tbsp	**liquid honey**	15 mL
1 tbsp	**butter**	15 mL
1/2 tsp	**dry mustard**	2 mL
Pinch	**each salt and white pepper**	Pinch

■ In saucepan of lightly salted boiling water, cook onions for 10 minutes. Drain and transfer to 6-cup (1.5 L) casserole.

■ Mix together ketchup, water, honey, butter, mustard, salt and pepper; pour over onions. Bake in 350°F (180°C) oven for 1 hour or until onions are tender and glazed. Makes 6 servings.

Crispy Onion Rings

You'll like the sweetness of these Spanish onion rings coated in this light batter.

2	**Spanish onions**	2
1 cup	**milk**	250 mL
3/4 tsp	**salt**	4 mL
1 cup	**all-purpose flour**	250 mL
1/4 tsp	**pepper**	1 mL
	Vegetable oil for deep-frying	

■ Cut onions into 1/4-inch (5 mm) thick slices; separate into rings.

■ In shallow bowl, stir together milk and 1/2 tsp (2 mL) of the salt; add onion rings and soak for 30 minutes, stirring occasionally.

■ In bag, combine flour, remaining salt and pepper. Add onion rings in batches and shake to coat.

■ In deep-fryer or large saucepan, heat 2 inches (5 cm) oil to 375°F (190°C) or until 1-inch (2.5 cm) cube of white bread turns golden brown in 40 seconds. Deep-fry rings, in batches and without crowding, for about 3 minutes or until golden brown. Drain and keep warm in paper towel-lined baking dish in 250°F (120°C) oven until serving on warm platter. Makes about 4 servings.

THE HONORABLE ONION
Onions can be star material for your menu planning. Boiled, baked or braised, they make a delicious side dish for roasts and chops. Raw, they're a flavorful ingredient for salads; deep-fried, they become a crunchy appetizer.
• The most popular variety is the domestic yellow cooking onion. It has a good full flavor and is available year-round. Choose firm onions and remember that the older the onion, the stronger the flavor.
• To remove onion odors from your hands after peeling, rub hands with lemon or salt; from a knife, rub with raw potato or lemon. To prevent tears when preparing onions, peel them under cold running water.

Tomatoes under the Sun

A delectable pesto dressing enhances the flavor of tomatoes. You can also finely chop instead of purée the basil, pine nuts, sun-dried tomatoes and garlic. This beautiful salad combines all the best flavors of summer.

4	**ripe tomatoes**	4
	Basil leaves	
	Lemon wedges	
	DRESSING	
1/4 cup	**coarsely chopped fresh basil**	50 mL
1/4 cup	**good-quality olive oil**	50 mL
4 tsp	**toasted pine nuts**	20 mL
2 tsp	**chopped sun-dried tomatoes, drained (optional)**	10 mL
1	**clove garlic**	1
2 tbsp	**lemon juice**	25 mL
	Salt and pepper	

■ Slice tomatoes and arrange on serving platter; set aside.

■ **Dressing:** In food processor fitted with metal blade, combine basil, oil, 2 tsp (10 mL) of the pine nuts, sun-dried tomatoes (if using) and garlic; process for 30 seconds. Add lemon juice, and salt and pepper to taste; process for 10 seconds or until well blended.

■ Pour over tomatoes; sprinkle with remaining pine nuts. Garnish with basil leaves and lemon wedges. Chill for 1 hour. Makes 6 servings.

Carrot Salad

Grating the carrots in a food processor makes this speedy recipe even quicker.

4	**large carrots**	4
3 tbsp	**lemon juice**	50 mL
3 tbsp	**vegetable oil**	50 mL
1 tsp	**granulated sugar**	5 mL
1 tsp	**Dijon mustard**	5 mL
1/4 tsp	**pepper**	1 mL
2 tbsp	**chopped fresh parsley**	25 mL
	Salt	
	Lettuce leaves	

■ Peel and grate carrots. In bowl, whisk together lemon juice, oil, sugar, mustard and pepper. Add carrots and parsley; toss to coat well. Cover and refrigerate until chilled or for up to 8 hours.

■ Toss salad and season with salt to taste; spoon onto lettuce-lined plates. Makes 4 servings.

Tomatoes under the Sun ▶

Pear-Ginger Waldorf Salad

Update a Waldorf salad by combining firm ripe pears, ginger and pecans with the more familiar ingredients. Serve this refreshing salad at a brunch with curried crêpes or on a buffet table.

2 cups	chopped pears (unpeeled)	500 mL
1 cup	chopped celery	250 mL
1/2 cup	chopped pecans	125 mL
1/2 cup	raisins	125 mL
	DRESSING	
1/2 cup	mayonnaise	125 mL
3 tbsp	lemon juice	50 mL
1/4 cup	finely chopped crystallized ginger	50 mL
	Salt and pepper	

■ In salad bowl, combine pears, celery, pecans and raisins.

■ **Dressing:** Mix together mayonnaise, lemon juice and ginger; season with salt and pepper to taste. Pour over salad and toss well. Serve immediately or refrigerate for up to 8 hours. Makes 4 to 6 servings.

Waldorf Salad

Use whatever green and red apples are in season. Swiss, Colby or brick cheeses go well in this salad.

2	red apples (unpeeled), diced	2
1	green apple (unpeeled), diced	1
1 tbsp	lemon juice	15 mL
1 cup	diced celery	250 mL
1 cup	seedless grapes, halved	250 mL
1/2 cup	shredded mild cheese	125 mL
1/4 cup	mayonnaise	50 mL
1/4 cup	sour cream	50 mL
1/2 cup	toasted slivered almonds	125 mL

■ In large bowl, sprinkle red and green apples with lemon juice. Add celery, grapes and cheese; toss to mix.

■ Combine mayonnaise with sour cream; pour over salad and toss to coat. Refrigerate until chilled. Add almonds; toss to mix. Makes 6 servings.

Spinach Salad with Creamy Dressing

Most spinach salads are served with a vinaigrette dressing. In this one, spinach and romaine lettuce are tossed with a creamy dressing.

1	small bunch spinach, trimmed	1
Half	small head romaine lettuce	Half
1/2 lb	bacon, cooked and crumbled	250 g
1/4 lb	mushrooms, sliced	125 g
2	hard-cooked eggs, chopped	2
	DRESSING	
2/3 cup	mayonnaise	150 mL
2 tbsp	chili sauce or ketchup	25 mL
2 tbsp	light or whipping cream	25 mL
1 tbsp	lemon juice	15 mL
1 tbsp	liquid honey	15 mL
	Salt and pepper	

■ Tear spinach and lettuce into bite-size pieces. In large bowl, combine spinach, lettuce, bacon, mushrooms and eggs.

■ **Dressing:** Combine mayonnaise, chili sauce, cream, lemon juice and honey; season with salt and pepper to taste. Pour over salad and toss to coat well. Makes 4 to 6 servings.

Cucumber-Tomato Chunky Cheese Salad with Jumbo Croutons

Bite-size cherry tomatoes in a crunchy, colorful make-ahead salad make perfect picnic fare for a crowd.

1/3 cup	olive oil	75 mL
1/4 cup	white wine vinegar	50 mL
2 tsp	chopped fresh basil	10 mL
1 tsp	chopped fresh oregano	5 mL
1/4 tsp	granulated sugar	1 mL
	Salt and pepper	
2	English cucumbers	2
1	large red onion	1
1	each sweet red and green pepper	1
3/4 lb	dilled Havarti cheese	375 g
20	jumbo pitted black olives	20
2 lb	cherry tomatoes	1 kg
1/4 cup	chopped fresh parsley	50 mL
	Jumbo Croutons (recipe follows)	

■ In large salad bowl, whisk together oil and vinegar; stir in basil, oregano, sugar, and salt and pepper to taste.

■ Trim cucumbers. With vegetable peeler, peel off strips 1/2 inch (1 cm) apart to create stripes. Cut into large chunks and add to bowl.

■ Slice onion thinly; add to bowl. Cut red and green peppers into 1/2-inch (1 cm) dice; add to bowl. Cut cheese into 1-inch (2.5 cm) cubes; quarter olives lengthwise. Add cheese and olives to bowl along with tomatoes and parsley; toss to combine. *(Salad can be covered and refrigerated for up to 12 hours.)* To serve, toss with croutons. Makes 12 to 16 servings.

JUMBO CROUTONS

6	thick slices Italian bread	6
1/4 cup	butter (preferably unsalted)	50 mL
2 tbsp	olive oil	25 mL
1	clove garlic, crushed	1
Pinch	dried thyme	Pinch

■ Cut bread into 1-inch (2.5 cm) cubes. In large skillet, melt butter with oil over medium-low heat; cook garlic and thyme for 5 minutes. Discard garlic. Add bread cubes and toss to coat; spread in shallow baking pan. Bake in 300°F (150°C) oven for 15 to 20 minutes or until crisp and golden, turning halfway through.

Egg Salad Mould

Everyone loves egg salad, and leftovers make great sandwiches for lunch or a picnic.

12	hard-cooked eggs	12
1 cup	finely chopped celery	250 mL
1 cup	mayonnaise	250 mL
1/2 cup	finely chopped gherkins	125 mL
1/3 cup	finely chopped onion	75 mL
1/4 cup	finely chopped fresh parsley	50 mL
1 tbsp	prepared mustard	15 mL
1 tsp	salt	5 mL
	Pepper	
1	pkg unflavored gelatin	1
1/3 cup	cold water	75 mL

■ In large bowl, mash eggs; stir in celery, mayonnaise, gherkins, onion, parsley, mustard, salt, and pepper to taste.

■ In saucepan, sprinkle gelatin over water; heat over low heat until dissolved. Pour into egg mixture and mix well. Turn into lightly oiled 8-cup (2 L) mould or 9- × 5-inch (2 L) loaf pan. Refrigerate until firm, at least 4 hours or overnight.

■ To unmould salad, loosen edge with knife; invert onto serving plate. Place hot damp cloth over mould; shake to release. Makes 10 to 12 servings.

Chicken Salad in Melon

Piled high with a fruited chicken salad mixture and served with homemade melba toast and iced tea, this delightful combination makes a refreshing luncheon dish. You'll find pink peppercorns at specialty food stores.

3	cantaloupes	3
3 cups	cubed cooked chicken	750 mL
1/2 cup	diagonally sliced celery	125 mL
3 tbsp	slivered chives	50 mL
1/2 cup	plain yogurt	125 mL
1/4 cup	raspberries, mashed	50 mL
1 tbsp	raspberry vinegar	15 mL
1/2 tsp	salt	2 mL
	Pink peppercorns	
	Raspberries	

■ Cut cantaloupes in half; remove seeds. With melon baller, scoop out pulp from two of the halves. In bowl, gently mix together chicken, celery, chives and melon balls.

■ Stir together yogurt, raspberries, vinegar and salt; add half to chicken mixture and toss to coat lightly.

■ To serve, spoon salad into remaining melon halves. Spoon remaining dressing over or pass separately. Garnish with peppercorns and raspberries. Makes 4 servings.

FRUIT VINEGARS

Our Chicken Salad in Melon recipe calls for raspberry vinegar. You can buy the bottled variety or make your own. It's very easy to make fruit vinegars. Here's how:

• Simply place 1 cup (250 mL) washed raspberries, strawberries, blueberries, red or black currants, or chopped peeled peaches or plums in a 2-cup (500 mL) sterilized Mason-type jar. Fill with plain white vinegar and seal. Let stand in a dark place for 2 to 3 weeks. Strain vinegar into sterilized jar and seal. Store in a cool dry place. Makes about 1 cup (250 mL).

Chutney Chicken Salad

Waldorf flavors meld beautifully with flavors of the Far East to enhance this chicken salad. Poach 2 lb (1 kg) of boneless chicken breasts to make 4 cups (1 L) cubed chicken.

4 cups	cubed cooked chicken	1 L
1 cup	chopped celery	250 mL
1/4 cup	chopped green onion	50 mL
2	apples, cubed	2
1/4 cup	raisins	50 mL
1/4 cup	white wine or orange juice	50 mL
2 tsp	curry powder	10 mL
3/4 cup	light mayonnaise	175 mL
1/4 cup	light sour cream	50 mL
2 tbsp	chutney	25 mL
2 tbsp	slivered preserved ginger	25 mL

■ In bowl, toss together chicken, celery, onion and apples.

■ In small saucepan, combine raisins, wine and curry powder; heat until raisins are plump. Pour over chicken mixture.

■ Combine mayonnaise, sour cream, chutney and ginger; pour over chicken mixture and stir gently to coat. Makes 6 servings.

Zesty Sauerkraut Salad

This German-type salad is good with bean dishes, ham, cold roast pork, sausages and hot dogs. To dilute the vinegary taste of the sauerkraut, drain, then rinse under cold water — the longer you rinse it, the milder the sauerkraut.

1	can (28 oz/796 mL) sauerkraut	1
1	carrot, grated	1
1/4 cup	chopped radishes or celery	50 mL
1/4 cup	finely chopped red or green onion	50 mL
1 tsp	dill seeds	5 mL
1/4 cup	vegetable oil	50 mL
1 tsp	granulated sugar	5 mL
	Salt and pepper	

■ In sieve, drain sauerkraut and rinse under cold water; drain. In salad bowl, combine sauerkraut, carrot, radishes, onion and dill seeds.

■ Mix oil with sugar until sugar has dissolved; pour over salad and toss to mix. Season with salt and pepper to taste. Serve immediately or cover and refrigerate for up to 4 days. Makes about 8 servings.

Lentil-Carrot Salad

This crunchy, colorful Mediterranean salad is nutritious, high in fibre and keeps well in the refrigerator for up to 3 days. Serve at room temperature.

1 cup	brown lentils	250 mL
1 cup	diced carrots	250 mL
2	large cloves garlic, minced	2
1	bay leaf	1
1/2 tsp	dried thyme	2 mL
1 cup	diced red onion	250 mL
1/2 cup	diced celery	125 mL
1/4 cup	chopped fresh parsley	50 mL
1/4 cup	olive oil	50 mL
1/4 cup	lemon juice	50 mL
1 tsp	salt	5 mL
1/4 tsp	pepper	1 mL

■ In saucepan, combine lentils, carrots, garlic, bay leaf and thyme; add enough water to cover by at least 1 inch (2.5 cm). Bring to boil; reduce heat and simmer, uncovered, for 15 to 20 minutes or until lentils are tender but not mushy. Drain; discard bay leaf.

■ Transfer to bowl. Add onion, celery, parsley, oil, lemon juice, salt and pepper; toss to mix. Let cool to room temperature. Makes 6 to 8 servings.

German-Style Potato and Sausage Salad

Pop sausage and foil-wrapped garlic onto the barbecue one evening as a head start for this salad the next day. If you can't find kielbasa, use wieners, leaving them whole, and grill for 3 to 5 minutes. Accompany with rye bread and a raw vegetable platter.

4	potatoes (about 1-1/2 lb/750 g), unpeeled	4
2 tbsp	white vinegar	25 mL
1	large dill pickle, coarsely chopped	1
1 tbsp	each finely chopped fresh parsley and onion	15 mL
1	head garlic	1
2 tsp	vegetable oil	10 mL
1 lb	smoked sausage (kielbasa)	500 g
1/2 cup	light mayonnaise	125 mL
1 tbsp	German-style mustard	15 mL
1/2 tsp	salt	2 mL
1/4 tsp	pepper	1 mL
	Tomato wedges	

■ In saucepan of boiling salted water, cook potatoes until tender; drain well. Peel (if desired) and slice. In large bowl, sprinkle warm potatoes with vinegar; stir in dill pickle, parsley and onion. Let cool.

■ Remove any loose papery layers from garlic head. Place on foil and drizzle with half of the oil; loosely wrap. Grill for 25 to 35 minutes or until softened, turning occasionally.

■ Peel sausage if necessary; cut in half lengthwise. Brush with remaining oil; grill for 15 to 20 minutes or until browned, turning occasionally. Slice and let cool; add to potatoes.

■ Squeeze roasted garlic into bowl, discarding any charred pieces; mash until smooth. Stir in mayonnaise, mustard, salt and pepper; pour over potatoes and toss. *(Salad can be covered and refrigerated for up to 1 day.)* Garnish with tomato wedges. Makes 4 servings.

TOMATO SALAD PROVENÇALE
Halve 2 tomatoes crosswise and scoop out seeds. Mix together 1/4 cup (50 mL) minced black olives, 1/4 cup (50 mL) minced celery and 4 tsp (20 mL) chopped fresh parsley; sprinkle over cut sides of tomatoes. Whisk together 2 tbsp (25 mL) olive oil, 2 tsp (10 mL) lemon juice, 1 minced clove garlic, and salt and pepper to taste; spoon over tomatoes. Garnish with strips of lemon rind. Makes 4 servings.

German-Style Potato and Sausage Salad ▶

occoli, Mushroom and Feta Cheese Salad

Serve this colorful winter salad as a first course or as a side dish with an omelette, soup, grilled meat or chicken. You can prepare the salad and refrigerate it overnight, but add the almonds just before serving.

1	**bunch broccoli**	1
1	**red onion, thinly sliced and separated into rings**	1
1/4 lb	**small mushrooms**	125 g
1/4 lb	**feta cheese, crumbled**	125 g
	Salt and pepper	
2 tbsp	**toasted sliced almonds**	25 mL
	VINAIGRETTE	
1/4 cup	**water**	50 mL
2 tbsp	**olive oil**	25 mL
2 tbsp	**lemon juice**	25 mL
1	**clove garlic, minced**	1
1/2 tsp	**dried oregano**	2 mL

■ Trim broccoli. Peel stalks and cut into 1- × 1/4-inch (2.5 cm × 5 mm) strips. Cut tops into bite-size florets.

■ In salad bowl, toss broccoli with onion, mushrooms and cheese.

■ **Vinaigrette:** Combine water, oil, lemon juice, garlic and oregano; pour over vegetables and toss to mix. Season with salt and pepper to taste; toss again. Sprinkle almonds over top. Makes about 8 servings.

TOMATO SALAD WITH FRESH HERBS
Peel and seed 4 tomatoes. Cut into large cubes and toss with 2 tbsp (25 mL) chopped fresh parsley, 1 tbsp (15 mL) chopped fresh chives, 1 tbsp (15 mL) chopped fresh basil or tarragon or 1 tsp (5 mL) rosemary or thyme, 1 minced clove garlic, 2 tbsp (25 mL) olive oil, and salt and pepper to taste. Serve immediately. Makes 4 servings.

Parsleyed Chick-Pea Salad

Canned chick-peas, or garbanzo beans, make a quick and satisfying salad base.
Chill in the refrigerator overnight for a full-bodied flavor.

1	can (19 oz/540 mL) chick-peas, drained	1
1/2 cup	chopped fresh parsley	125 mL
1	sweet red or green pepper, diced (optional)	1
2 tbsp	finely chopped red onion	25 mL
2	cloves garlic, minced	2
1/4 cup	olive oil	50 mL
1 tbsp	(approx) lemon juice	15 mL
	Salt and pepper	
	Cherry tomatoes (optional)	

■ In salad bowl, combine chick-peas, parsley, red pepper (if using), onion, garlic, oil, lemon juice, and salt and pepper to taste; toss well. Chill for at least 2 hours or overnight to blend flavors.

■ Taste and adjust seasoning; add more lemon juice if desired. Garnish with cherry tomatoes (if using). Makes 4 servings.

OVERNIGHT SALADS

Busy cooks always appreciate the convenience of make-ahead foods. And what better way to make meal planning easier than having a salad ready and waiting in the refrigerator? With these two easy prepare-the-night-before salads, you can add a new dimension to a family meal of soup, sandwiches, hamburgers or chops. They're ideal for buffet tables, lunch-boxes and picnics.

Grilled Antipasto Salad Platter

Barbecue the vegetables for this colorful salad a day ahead, then marinate them overnight in an easy dressing. Serve with cold meat and cheese for a delicious garlic-lover's meal.

1	jar (6 oz/170 mL) marinated artichoke hearts	1
3	cloves garlic, minced	3
1/4 tsp	each salt and dried oregano	1 mL
1	eggplant (about 3/4 lb/375 g)	1
	Salt	
1	sweet red, green or yellow pepper	1
2	small zucchini (or 1 zucchini and 1 yellow squash)	2
2 tbsp	olive oil	25 mL
	Leaf lettuce	
8	thin slices salami	8
8	thin slices mozzarella cheese	8
	Tomato wedges	
	Black olives	

■ Drain artichoke hearts, reserving liquid in bowl; stir in garlic, salt and oregano. Set aside. Return artichoke hearts to jar and refrigerate.

■ Cut eggplant into 1/2-inch (1 cm) thick slices. Place in sieve; sprinkle lightly with salt and let drain for 30 minutes. Rinse and pat dry.

■ Meanwhile, grill pepper, turning often, until charred all over, 15 to 20 minutes. Cover with tea towel and let stand for 10 minutes; peel off charred skin and cut into 6 strips.

■ Cut zucchini in half lengthwise. Brush zucchini and eggplant with oil; grill for 5 to 8 minutes per side or until tender and golden brown but not charred. Place grilled red pepper, zucchini and eggplant in large bowl.

■ Whisk any remaining oil into reserved garlic mixture; taste and adjust seasoning if necessary. Pour over vegetables and stir to coat. Cover and refrigerate for at least 8 or up to 24 hours, stirring occasionally.

■ To serve, bring vegetables to room temperature. Arrange on large lettuce-lined platter along with salami, cheese, artichoke hearts, tomatoes and olives. Makes 4 servings.

Main-Course Vegetable Pasta Salad

Serve this colorful salad along with a hot soup for a delightful supper. Or serve it with a variety of cold meats and omit the meat in the salad. If you're short of time, don't broil the peppers, although they'll have less flavor.

1	each sweet red and yellow pepper	1
4 cups	radiatore, rotini, fusilli or other small pasta	1 L
1	large tomato, sliced	1
Half	English cucumber, sliced	Half
5 oz	salami, cooked beef or chicken, cut in strips	150 g
1/2 cup	cubed Cheddar or feta cheese	125 mL
1/2 cup	pitted black olives	125 mL
	VINAIGRETTE	
2	large cloves garlic, minced	2
1/2 cup	white wine vinegar	125 mL
2 tsp	Dijon mustard	10 mL
1/2 tsp	salt	2 mL
1-1/4 cups	vegetable oil	300 mL

■ Broil red and yellow peppers, turning often, until blackened and blistered, about 10 minutes. Let cool for 10 minutes; peel off charred skin and cut into thin strips.

■ In large pot of boiling salted water, cook pasta until tender but firm; drain.

■ **Vinaigrette:** In food processor or bowl, combine garlic, vinegar, mustard and salt; with machine running, gradually pour in oil in thin steady stream. Toss 1/2 cup (125 mL) with pasta; spread on serving platter or individual plates.

■ Toss red and yellow peppers with 1/2 cup (125 mL) vinaigrette. Attractively arrange red and yellow peppers, tomato, cucumber, salami, cheese and olives over pasta; drizzle lightly with vinaigrette. Pass remaining vinaigrette separately.

Makes 4 main-course servings.

Green Beans with Tuna Mayonnaise

Tonnato is a classic tuna mayonnaise spread for cold veal and, more recently, for turkey and chicken breasts. It's delicious with crisp cooked beans arranged over romaine lettuce hearts, then garnished with tomato slices and black olives.

1 lb	green beans, trimmed	500 g
6	leaves romaine lettuce (heart only)	6
2	tomatoes	2
12	black olives	12
1 tbsp	tiny capers	15 mL
	Chopped fresh basil	
	TUNA MAYONNAISE	
1 cup	light mayonnaise	250 mL
1/3 cup	mashed drained solid white tuna	75 mL
2 tbsp	plain yogurt	25 mL
1 tbsp	lemon juice	15 mL

■ In large saucepan of boiling salted water, cook beans until tender-crisp, 5 to 8 minutes. Drain and refresh under cold water; pat dry. Arrange along with lettuce leaves around centre of large oval platter. Cut tomatoes into slices from tops to bottoms; set aside.

■ **Tuna Mayonnaise:** In small bowl, combine mayonnaise, tuna, yogurt and lemon juice; taste and adjust seasoning if necessary. Place in centre of bean platter; arrange tomato slices and olives around beans. Garnish mayonnaise with capers; garnish vegetables with basil. Serve immediately. Makes 4 servings.

> *COMPOSED SALAD OF GREEN BEANS, TOMATOES AND CUCUMBERS*
> *Marinate 3/4 lb (375 g) cooked tender-crisp green beans in 1/2 cup (125 mL) of your favorite vinaigrette for 1 hour. Remove with slotted spoon to serving platter. Arrange 3 sliced tomatoes on one side and half a sliced English cucumber on the other. Drizzle with dressing. Makes 4 servings.*

Zucchini Slaw

Unique and colorful, this slaw will become a summer favorite. Salting and draining the zucchini will prevent excess liquid from watering down the dressing.

6	medium zucchini, grated (about 1-1/2 lb/750 g)	6
2 tsp	salt	10 mL
1	large carrot, grated	1
1	sweet red pepper, julienned	1
1	red onion, thinly sliced	1
1	stalk celery, julienned	1
2 tbsp	each chopped fresh parsley and dill	25 mL

DRESSING		
3/4 cup	mayonnaise	175 mL
2 tbsp	Dijon mustard	25 mL
2 tbsp	red wine vinegar	25 mL
1 tbsp	olive oil	15 mL
1 tbsp	liquid honey	15 mL
1 tsp	horseradish	5 mL
1/4 tsp	pepper	1 mL

■ Combine zucchini and salt; toss well. Place in colander; let stand for 30 minutes. Rinse under cold water; drain and squeeze out excess moisture.

■ Place zucchini in bowl and add carrot, red pepper, onion and celery; toss well. Sprinkle with parsley and dill.

■ **Dressing:** Combine mayonnaise, mustard, vinegar, oil, honey, horseradish and pepper; stir into zucchini mixture. Taste and adjust seasoning if necessary. Makes 6 to 8 servings.

Picnic Pasta Salad

This hearty make-ahead salad is sure to become a favorite for a crowd.

5 cups	route (cartwheel pasta) or fusilli	1.25 L
1/2 cup	olive or vegetable oil	125 mL
Pinch	nutmeg	Pinch
1 cup	fresh peas	250 mL
3 tbsp	each finely chopped fresh parsley and dill	50 mL
1 tbsp	chopped fresh basil	15 mL
3 tbsp	red wine vinegar	50 mL
1 tbsp	lemon juice	15 mL
1 tsp	Dijon mustard	5 mL
	Salt and pepper	
5	baby zucchini, thinly sliced	5
1/2 cup	snipped fresh chives	125 mL

■ In large saucepan of lightly salted boiling water, cook pasta until tender but firm; drain well. Add 2 tbsp (25 mL) of the oil; toss to coat. Sprinkle with nutmeg; toss and let cool.

■ In saucepan of lightly salted boiling water, blanch peas for 1 to 2 minutes or just until tender; drain well and set aside.

■ Pour remaining oil into large salad bowl; stir in parsley, dill and basil. Whisk in vinegar, lemon juice, mustard, and salt and pepper to taste. Add cooled pasta, peas, zucchini and chives; toss well. Cover and refrigerate until chilled or for up to 12 hours. Makes 12 to 16 servings.

PASTA SALADS

Use any one of several small pasta shapes in Picnic Pasta Salad or Main-Course Vegetable Pasta Salad (p. 50). Choose from farfalle (small bows), penne (like quill pens), elbows, route (cartwheels), fusilli (long spirals), or rotini (small spirals). Colored pasta — spinach, basil, tomato or whole wheat — makes a pleasant change as well.

• Remember to cook until al dente (tender but firm) and drain well.

Springtime Salad

This lovely salad has all the fresh tastes of spring.

2 cups	fiddleheads	500 mL
1/2 lb	asparagus	250 g
1/3 cup	olive oil	75 mL
1 cup	small mushrooms, trimmed (4 oz/125 g)	250 mL
	Salt	
2	hard-cooked eggs	2
2 tbsp	white wine vinegar	25 mL
1 tsp	Dijon mustard	5 mL
	Pepper	
1 tbsp	snipped chives	15 mL
	Leaf or Boston lettuce leaves	

■ In separate saucepans, steam or boil fiddleheads and asparagus until tender-crisp, 4 to 5 minutes. Drain and rinse under cold water; drain well and set aside.

■ In small skillet, heat 2 tbsp (25 mL) of the oil over medium-high heat; sauté mushrooms and pinch of salt for 3 minutes or until light golden. Set aside.

■ Separate whites from yolks; dice whites finely and set aside. In small bowl, mash yolks; blend in vinegar, mustard, remaining oil, and salt and pepper to taste. Stir in chives.

■ Arrange lettuce on large platter; arrange fiddleheads over top. Fan asparagus on top of fiddleheads; mound mushrooms at base. Sprinkle with egg whites; pour dressing over salad. Makes 4 to 6 servings.

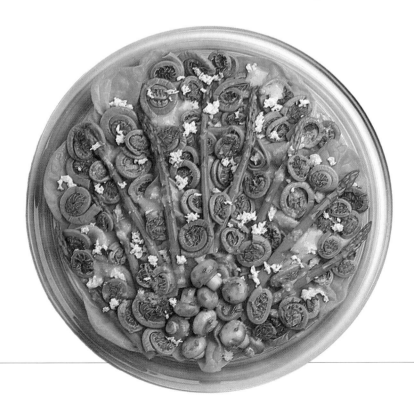

Salsa Salad in Lettuce Cups

A refreshing partner for chili burgers is this delicious avocado and tomato salad, pepped up with hot peppers and given a south-of-the-border twist with fresh coriander. Add parsley and more peppers if fresh coriander isn't available.

1-1/2 cups	chopped tomatoes	375 mL
1 cup	diced peeled avocado	250 mL
1/2 cup	diced seeded cucumber	125 mL
1/4 cup	diced red onion	50 mL
1/4 cup	minced fresh coriander	50 mL
1/4 cup	olive oil	50 mL
2 tbsp	lime juice	25 mL
1 tbsp	(approx) minced jalapeño pepper	15 mL
1	clove garlic, minced	1
1/4 tsp	each salt and pepper	1 mL
1	small head Boston lettuce, separated	1
	Chopped fresh coriander	

■ In bowl, gently stir together tomatoes, avocado, cucumber, onion, minced coriander, oil, lime juice, jalapeño pepper, garlic, salt and pepper. Taste and adjust seasoning, adding more jalapeño pepper if desired.

■ Discard coarse outer leaves from lettuce. Arrange lettuce cups on salad plates; fill with salad. Garnish with coriander. Makes about 4 servings.

Technicolor Summer Slaw

This brightly colored seven-vegetable slaw goes wonderfully with burgers.

4 cups	shredded green cabbage	1 L
2 cups	shredded red cabbage	500 mL
1	carrot, shredded	1
1/2 cup	each diced sweet red and green pepper	125 mL
1/4 cup	diced celery	50 mL
1/4 cup	minced green onions	50 mL
1/2 cup	light mayonnaise	125 mL
1/3 cup	low-fat plain yogurt	75 mL
1 tsp	Dijon mustard	5 mL
1/2 tsp	horseradish	2 mL
1/4 tsp	each salt and pepper	1 mL

■ In salad bowl, toss together green and red cabbages, carrot, red and green peppers, celery and onions.

■ Stir together mayonnaise, yogurt, mustard, horseradish, salt and pepper; toss with cabbage mixture to coat evenly. Taste and adjust seasoning. Makes about 4 servings.

Gazpacho Salad

Serve this with sour cream and chives for a change from mayonnaise.

2	pkg unflavored gelatin	2
2-1/2 cups	tomato or vegetable juice	625 mL
2 tbsp	wine vinegar	25 mL
1 tbsp	packed brown sugar	15 mL
1 tsp	salt	5 mL
1 tsp	Worcestershire sauce	5 mL
Dash	hot pepper sauce	Dash
1	small clove garlic, minced	1
2	tomatoes, peeled, seeded and diced	2
1 cup	chopped peeled cucumber	250 mL
1/2 cup	diced sweet green pepper	125 mL
1/4 cup	chopped green onion	50 mL
	Lettuce	
	Thin slices cucumber	

■ In saucepan over medium heat, sprinkle gelatin over 1/2 cup (125 mL) of the tomato juice to dissolve. (Or, in microwaveable bowl, sprinkle gelatin over 1/2 cup/125 mL of the tomato juice; microwave at High for 1 minute or until dissolved.) Add remaining tomato juice, vinegar, sugar, salt, Worcestershire sauce, hot pepper sauce and garlic. Chill until slightly thickened and consistency of egg whites.

■ Meanwhile, mix together tomatoes, cucumber, green pepper and onion; fold into thickened juice mixture. Pour into rinsed or greased 6-cup (1.5 L) mould. Chill until firm.

■ To serve, unmould onto lettuce-lined plate; garnish with cucumber. Makes 6 servings.

CREAMY CUCUMBER SALAD
In bowl, combine 1 sliced seedless cucumber, 1 finely chopped green onion, 1 cup (250 mL) sour cream, 1 tbsp (15 mL) chopped fresh dill and 1/2 tsp (2 mL) salt. Chill thoroughly. Makes 4 to 6 servings.

Warm Caesar Potato Salad

The potato is one of the most versatile and economical of salad ingredients. This dish is an ideal accompaniment to any grilled meat.

6	red potatoes (unpeeled)	6
1	small head romaine lettuce	1
1/2 cup	olive oil	125 mL
1	clove garlic, minced	1
1/4 cup	lemon juice	50 mL
2 tbsp	finely chopped fresh parsley	25 mL
2 tsp	Worcestershire sauce	10 mL
1 tsp	prepared mustard	5 mL
	Salt and pepper	
1/4 cup	freshly grated Parmesan cheese	50 mL
3/4 cup	garlic croutons	175 mL

■ In pot of boiling salted water, cook potatoes just until tender, about 20 minutes. Drain and let cool slightly; peel and cut into 1/2-inch (1 cm) cubes. Set aside.

■ Tear lettuce into bite-size pieces; place in large salad bowl and set aside.

■ In large skillet, heat oil over medium heat; cook garlic for 2 minutes. Stir in lemon juice, parsley, Worcestershire, mustard, and salt and pepper to taste.

■ Stir in diced potatoes; cook over medium-high heat for 2 minutes, stirring constantly. Pour over lettuce and toss well. Sprinkle with Parmesan and toss again. Arrange on individual salad plates; top with garlic croutons. Serve immediately. Makes 6 servings.

Oriental Dressing

Enjoy this zesty dressing on a fresh spinach salad or a combination of greens.

1/3 cup	rice vinegar	75 mL
1 tbsp	granulated sugar	15 mL
1 tbsp	finely chopped green onion	15 mL
1 tbsp	soy sauce	15 mL
1 tsp	Worcestershire sauce	5 mL
1	large clove garlic, minced	1
1/4 tsp	finely grated gingerroot	1 mL
	Salt and pepper	
2/3 cup	vegetable or peanut oil	150 mL

■ In small bowl, combine vinegar, sugar, onion, soy sauce, Worcestershire sauce, garlic, gingerroot, and salt and pepper to taste. Gradually whisk in oil. Let stand for up to 1 hour for flavors to blend. Whisk again. Makes 1-1/4 cups (300 mL).

Classic Vinaigrette

Keep this dressing on hand in the refrigerator to use on a variety of salads.
Chopped tarragon, parsley or chives add a fresh touch.

1/4 cup	wine vinegar	50 mL
1 tsp	Dijon mustard	5 mL
3/4 tsp	salt	4 mL
	Pepper	
1	clove garlic, crushed	1
3/4 cup	vegetable oil	175 mL
1 tbsp	chopped fresh herbs (optional)	15 mL

■ In small bowl, combine vinegar, mustard, salt, pepper to taste and garlic; gradually whisk in oil. Add herbs (if using). Makes 1 cup (250 mL).

Italian Dressing

Try this zippy dressing for tomato and cucumber salads and other raw or cooked vegetable combinations. For a delicious garnish, sprinkle on thinly sliced oranges and red onions.

2 tbsp	white or red wine vinegar	25 mL
1 tbsp	finely chopped shallot or onion	15 mL
1 tbsp	lemon juice	15 mL
1-1/2 tsp	finely chopped fresh oregano (or 1/2 tsp/2 mL dried)	7 mL
1 tsp	finely chopped garlic	5 mL
1/2 tsp	salt	2 mL
	Pepper	
	Crushed red chilies	
1/3 cup	olive oil	75 mL

■ In small bowl, combine vinegar, shallot, lemon juice, oregano, garlic, salt, and pepper and chilies to taste. Gradually whisk in oil. Let stand for 1 hour for flavors to blend. Whisk again. Makes 2/3 cup (150 mL).

INSTANT SALAD BAR

For the most versatile salad bar, plan to buy vegetables, fruits and cheeses in amounts that allow enough variety, but a minimum of leftovers. Chill all ingredients until ready to serve.

Large salad bowl: Combine an interesting variety of salad greens, washed, chilled and torn in bite-size pieces. Here are some suggestions:

- *Iceberg lettuce*
  - *Romaine lettuce*
    - *Spinach leaves*
      - *Shredded cabbage*
        - *Endive*
        Additions: In small bowls, place an assortment of crunchy vegetables, fruit and cheeses so

guests can choose their favorites. Here are some choices:

- *Bean sprouts, rinsed in cold water*
- *Carrots, cut in julienne sticks*
- *Celery, chopped, crisped in cold water and drained*
- *Mushrooms, thinly sliced*
- *Spanish onion, sliced in rings*
- *Cucumber, sliced*
- *Tomatoes, cut in wedges*
- *Green grapes, cut in small bunches*
- *Cantaloupe, seeded and cut in wedges*
- *Assorted cheese wedges and chunks*

Toppings:

- *Croutons*
- *Grated Parmesan cheese*
- *Salad dressings*

Chunky Roquefort Dressing

If you prefer a piquant dressing, you'll love this one.

1/2 cup	vegetable oil	125 mL
1/4 cup	white wine vinegar	50 mL
2 tbsp	milk or light cream	25 mL
1/4 tsp	salt	1 mL
	Pepper	
1/4 cup	crumbled Roquefort or blue cheese	50 mL

■ In bowl, beat together oil, vinegar, milk, salt, and pepper to taste; gently stir in cheese. Refrigerate until thoroughly chilled. Makes about 1 cup (250 mL).

Buttermilk Herb Dressing

This dressing is delicious drizzled over a composed salad of green beans, red peppers and lettuce, or tossed with a lettuce or spinach salad.

1 cup	buttermilk	250 mL
1/4 cup	vegetable oil	50 mL
1 tbsp	finely chopped fresh parsley	15 mL
1 tbsp	finely chopped fresh dill (or 1/2 tsp/2 mL dried dillweed)	15 mL
1 tbsp	white wine vinegar	15 mL
1 tsp	Dijon mustard	5 mL
1/2 tsp	salt	2 mL
1	small clove garlic, minced	1

■ In food processor or jar with lid, combine buttermilk, oil, parsley, dill, vinegar, mustard, salt and garlic; process or shake to mix well. Makes about 1-1/4 cups (300 mL).